CW01086317

Soul
Waves

Soul Waves

an inspiring collection of writings
to bring peace to the waters within

Nikki Banas

Soul Waves

Copyright © 2021 Nikki Banas

All rights reserved. No portion of this book may be reproduced, stored in a retrieval system, or transmitted in any form or by any means— electronic, mechanical, photocopy, recording, or any other— except for brief quotations in printed reviews, without the prior permission of the publisher.

ISBN 9798746748539 paperback

Cover Photo: Copyright © Daisy on Instagram @daisyalisaa

for you—

may these words bring peace to the waves within your soul

Contents

I. Worth

today, may you remember…

Each new day holds its own special magic and possibility. *Every. Single. One.*

A single day holds the power to change *everything*. Today could be the day that you own your power and *you* change things for the better. If you have been thinking about doing something for yourself or your life— if you have been waiting for a sign to own your power and change your life for the better, *this is it.*

No matter what happened yesterday,
you can begin again brand new today. If you want to keep yesterday behind you, you can. *Step bravely into today.*

This day might hold what you have been waiting *so* long for. The answers to the questions you have been asking. The peace you have been seeking. The grace to move ahead. *Let today teach you what you need to learn.*

No matter what yesterday held,
today holds brand new joys, miracles, and love that are all waiting for you. *Claim them.*

begin again

Begin each day with a practice of centering your heart and soul. Do not rush into the obligations of the day without calming your spirit first. Remember that before everything else— every appointment, every obligation, every task— you are worthy of feeling peace and calm within your soul first.

Whether it is through a few quiet moments of meditation or a small walk outside, begin each day with a peaceful heart and a calm spirit. Find what brings you overwhelming peace, and honor your soul by gifting it to yourself before the day ahead.

No matter what happened yesterday— no matter what storms or sunshine you held— begin again by grounding yourself in the present moment. Begin again with love and gratitude for yesterday— for the memories of the bright sun or for the lessons from the storm. Begin again, knowing today is full of new possibilities and new opportunities. Begin again, welcoming new joys and new ways to love. With each new sunrise, begin again with a peaceful heart and a calm spirit.

divinely enough

You are enough. And not just enough, but *so much more* than enough. For all that you have been and all that you will become. All that you are today, in this moment of now, is more than enough. As a human. As a friend. As a spouse. As a parent. As a healer. As a giver. As a lover. You are enough in *all* that you are.

And it cannot be said enough. Your efforts— whether noticed and appreciated or not— are enough. There is only one requisite for being enough and it is in the *being*. You are here and that is enough. You are here, giving what you can, trying your best, and putting in your efforts day in and day out— know that that is enough.

You do not need to prove yourself because there is simply nothing to prove.

You do not need to change yourself in order to be enough. Your waters are not too deep, you are not too emotional. You do not need to change your personality. You are not too much anything.

You are simply, *divinely enough.*

Like every mountain, every yellow rose, every passing cloud, every wave in the ocean, and every shell on the beach holds its own divine place in our world, *you* hold a divine place in it all too. The story of our world would be incomplete without *you*— the real and authentic you. The you that simply is you. *You* are a divine part of it all.

divinely enough part 2— authentic growth

And the thing that we have backwards is that we think that once we are enough we will stop growing. That once we become enough we will somehow be 'done.' Once we graduate. Once we get the job. Once we get the house. Once we look a certain way... So we put ourselves in these loops of not being enough of *something*. Not smart enough. Not hard working enough. Not the right shape or size. Not loving enough...

But the truth is, real growth *begins* the moment you realize that you are, and always have been, enough.

When you stop working to just be enough— to squeeze yourself to fit into some mold of what you think you need to be like— and instead, realize that you are already enough, you grow from a place of authentic love for yourself instead.

You stop growing from a place of *proving*. You no longer try so hard to justify your place. You no longer grow from a place of *fear*— the fear of not being good enough. The fear of not fitting in because you are too much or too little of something. You stop growing from a place of *desperation*.

And it will just click one day. That you never needed to prove anything. That you were always enough. That you will *always* be enough. It is freeing. It is releasing. It is setting down expectations that were never yours to reach for, and instead reaching towards dreams that *are* yours to reach for.

When you remember that you are divinely enough just as you are, you grow and flourish in all of the ways *you* are meant to bloom. You stop growing from a place of fear or desperation, and instead, from a place of authenticity, inspiration, excitement, and possibility for what *you* truly want to grow into. And my beautiful friend, *that* is when your true colors will shine brighter than you could have ever imagined.

there is space for you

There is enough space for you, and for each and every one of us. The universe is plentiful and abundant, and is large enough for us all. You do not need to wonder or worry about if there is space for you. *There is.* There is enough space for every flower, every cloud, every animal, every mountain and every desert. And there is enough space for you, too. You are not too much or too little. You are not too loud or too quiet. You are not too different. You are not too anything. There is space meant just for you and your unique song that you sing in the world. There is space for who you have been, who you are, and who you want to be. Sing your unique song, set your soul free. My beautiful friend, *own your space.*

becoming you

Become the you that you so deeply desire to become. Become the you who inspires you. The you that makes you excited for *life*. Become the you that believes in yourself entirely, without hesitation or doubt. Become the you that bets on you, *every. single. time.* Become the you that lives out your dreams, the you that isn't afraid to change your life or take a leap of faith, because you know that you are meant for something more. Become the you that is the greatest version of yourself— the you that is strong and confident and beautiful in your own skin. Take the steps. Do what the best version of you would do... Become the you that you so deeply desire to become.

Soul Waves

a grounding practice

Every now and again,
go outside to sit in the grass
or the sand or the dirt
to just sit.
To just be and breathe.
To see how the earth moves.
To watch a little bird.
To watch a ladybug.
To witness a falling leaf and the gentle breeze.

Every now and again,
let yourself witness how the beautiful earth lives—
without worry of the past,
without worry of the future.
It just moves.
Every plant and animal lives and grows and moves
through the seasons,
just one breath at a time.
Just one moment at a time.
The more you witness how our greatest teacher lives,
the more you will see too,
that all there is to living,
is to live just one breath—
one moment—
at a time.

nature healing

Never underestimate the healing and restorative power of nature. With how quickly the world moves and how much time is given to screens, meetings, and sitting indoors, it can be easy to forget the magic found right outside the door to our natural world.

The peace in an afternoon walk under the sun. The calmness in allowing the breeze to blow through an open window onto your face. The stillness of a hike through a quiet forest. The coolness on your skin when jumping into a lake on a summer's day. The vastness of gazing up at a sky full of stars.

When you are tired, go into nature to awaken your spirit. When you have been moving too quickly and doing too many things too quickly, turn to the stillness of nature. When you are hurting, go to the unhurried and healing pace of our earth. *She will heal and awaken your spirit.*

checking in with yourself

Sometimes you do not realize how thirsty you are until you taste that first refreshing, cool sip of water. Sometimes you do not realize how exhausted your body is until you allow yourself uninterrupted rest. Sometimes you do not realize the weight you have been carrying until you finally set it all down. Sometimes you do not realize how fast you have been moving until you sit in stillness...

Check in with yourself. Are you getting the rest you need? Are you nurturing your body with all that it needs so that it can keep up with all that you do? Are you getting the time you need for yourself? Or are you giving so much time to others that you haven't had any time to spare for yourself? Have you healed and forgiven the things you need to in order to truly move ahead and live fully today? Have you done the things that light you up lately? Have you laughed so hard your belly ached recently? Have you checked in with where you are and where you want to go?

Check in with yourself often, my beautiful friend. Stay intentional and give yourself what you need to flourish.

rest and reawakening

One of the greatest things you could do for your soul is to understand when it needs true *rest* and when it needs to be *reawakened* because both can lead to feelings of exhaustion… Both can dim the light of life.

When you are tired, allow your mind, body, and soul to truly *rest*. Turn off the tv, shut off any distractions, and rest without guilt. Let yourself pause from the busy days to sink into the present moment full of peace. Allow yourself to relax all of your muscles and release all of the tension that you have been carrying.

And when your soul needs to be awakened, return to the things that *ignite* you— whether bathing in the sunshine, running in the sand, reading poetry, singing to your favorite songs, enjoying your favorite meal at your favorite restaurant, or learning something new… Go back to what ignites you. Go back to the things that make you happiest to be alive.

Whether your soul needs rest or it needs to be reignited, learn to understand what your soul is aching for and allow yourself all that it needs.

Soul Waves

honoring your needs

You are worthy of honoring your needs.
You are worthy of nourishment for your body,
and nourishment for your soul.
You are worthy of filling your cup
and reigniting your soul.
You are worthy of healing your wounds
and letting go of your past.
You are worthy of celebrating yourself.
You are worthy of becoming all that you want and need.

honoring your sacredness

Your soul is sacred. Your heart is sacred. Your body is sacred. Your mind is sacred. *You* are sacred. Your life is sacred. The way you spend your time and energy is sacred. To honor your sacredness is to treasure the precious gift of life.

Honor your body. Your soul's sacred home. Your body that allows you to do what you love and move through life. Honor your body with rest and nourishment. Movement and water. Gift your body with nourishing and energizing foods. Gift your body with the rest it truly needs. Go to bed with enough time for your body to get the deep rest and recovery that it needs with all that it does each day. Gift your body with the movement it was made to do— whether stretching or walking or dancing or swimming. *Honor your body as your soul's sacred home.*

Honor your mind. Tend to your thoughts. Fill your mind with thoughts of kindness and love towards yourself. When your mind is racing and overwhelmed, fill your mind with the thoughts that bring you peace. Think of your favorite moments. Think of people and things you love. Remind yourself that you are doing better than you think. *Honor your mind.*

Honor your soul. Your soul is meant to be full of passion. The fire inside of you is meant to burn strong and free. So honor your soul by doing things that help your fire burn— the things that make you come *alive*. The things that make you so happy that you just cannot contain the joy within you. Love. Family. Friends. Nature. Music. Art... The things that make your soul come alive and overflow with passion, the things that make you happy to be a human, the things that make you remember how beautiful and special this life really is— make more time for *those things. Honor your soul.*

Honor your energy. Spend more time with the people who refresh and recharge you. Spend less time with those who drain your spirit. Do more things that feel right and less of the things that feel wrong. Trust your intuition with people, places, and situations. Your intuition knows things before your mind can process them with logic. If something feels off, trust that feeling and move on. If something feels right, trust that feeling and dive in. Trust the energy around you and honor it by pouring into the things that uplift you.

Honor your space. Make it a priority to fill the spaces that you spend most of your time in with beauty. Even if you are living someplace temporarily, it is worth it to make it feel your own even in a small way. Take the time to add things to your spaces that make you smile and remind you of your purpose. Make them spaces that you love. Live in a place that inspires *you*. Live in a space that is beautiful to *you*.

Your soul is sacred. Your heart is sacred. Your body is sacred. Your mind is sacred. You are sacred. Your life is sacred. The way you spend your time and energy is sacred. To honor your sacredness is to treasure the precious gift of life.

II. Joy

a blessing

It is truly a blessing to be here. To be alive. To be able to *feel*. To be able to smile and sing and dance and celebrate and love and rejoice. To be able to cry and ache and hurt too. It is all a blessing... To be able to experience the seasons of life. To be able to ride the ups and downs that life brings. To grow and change as our lives grow and change. So celebrate the blessings that each day brings. Become really intentional about how you spend your days. Let the joy into your heart. Feel deeply and love freely. Let go and release the hurts sooner. Wonder more. Explore more. Stay in your comfort zone a little less. Do the things you dream of. Be brave. Be kind. Cherish each day's blessings.

inner light

Make it a practice to look for the light. Make it a practice to celebrate the good things. Make it a practice to become intentional about joy... Stop replaying the moments you regret. Stop replaying the moments when you made a mistake. Stop replaying the storms. Stop replaying the hurts. Start to replay the good memories instead. Replay the moments of joy. Replay the moments that light up your entire world. Replay the moments that you are so proud of... Fill your inner world with the good things. Fill your inner world with the things you love about yourself. Fill your inner world with the moments you felt like you were on top of the world. Fill your inner world with your ideas and your dreams and your plans.

Make it a practice to nourish your inner world because it will change how you see the world around you... You'll begin to look for the light more. *And you'll find it more.* You will feel lighter because there is an abundance of light to find as soon as you start looking for it. *It all starts with the light inside of you.* So let in the light, my beautiful friend. Let your world shine from within.

Soul Waves

better what ifs

What if this works out even better
than you thought possible?

What if the things that are not working out well truly
are making space for things far, far greater?

What if you trusted your gut and just went for it?

What if you succeed beyond your wildest dreams?

What if you made today the best day of your life?

What if you are far braver and stronger than you realize?

What if I told you that you *really, truly* could do this?

simple pleasures and little treasures

May you never forget to savor
the simple pleasures, the little treasures of life—
the blessings of being human.

Listening to old favorite songs.
Listening to a new song that you know
will become a new favorite.
Visiting new places.
Reading or watching a story
that touches your heart.
Meeting someone who makes
your heart skip a beat.

The sun painted in oranges and pinks
in the evening sky.
The first daffodils blooming
after the long winter.
The first cool day
after a long, hot summer.
The ocean's calm
before a stormy afternoon.
The warmth of the touch
from someone you love.
The softness and tenderness
of talking late through the night.

more of…

The things that light you up.
The places that make you fall in love.
The people who open your eyes
and ignite your heart.
The books that change the way you think.
The songs that you cannot help but sing along with.
The movies that touch your heart.
The food that fills you with energy.
The movement that fills your spirit with joy.
The dreams and ideas that you
cannot stop thinking about.
The things that fill up your cup.

More of…
Everything that makes you fall more in love with life.

the best days

The best days of life are not always the ones with grand excitement or thrilling triumph. They are often the ones full of sweet things and sweet moments. Slow mornings and un-rushed love. Little pleasures and nowhere to hurry to… The best days are often the ones with beautiful moments, one after the next, filling the day softly, *entirely*.

how to begin each day

Every day, begin with a grateful heart.
Begin with gratitude for what yesterday brought and
for all that today will bring.
Begin with a grateful heart for all of the people and
things in your life that you love.
Begin with gratitude for a brand new day,
for more time to do what you love,
and for more time to grow.
Every day, begin with a grateful heart for a new day to
experience this *life*.

how to end each day

Every day, end with a grateful heart.
Lay your head down on your pillow with gratitude
for all that the day brought you.
End the day with a grateful heart
for the experience of another day.
End the day with gratitude for the joys the day brought,
for the people you got to share the day with,
and for the love you felt.
End the day with a grateful heart
for the lessons you learned and the strength you found.
Every day, lay your head down on your pillow
with a grateful heart for a new day of
experiencing this *life*.

rushing towards the future

There is no need to rush towards *anything*. There is no race towards *anything*. There is nothing to rush towards... This moment holds so much breathtaking life for you. *This* moment— here and now. Slow down, and allow yourself to breathe in this moment. Slow down, and let yourself really see and feel all that is happening right now. The moments ahead that you are eager and excited for *will* come. But until they do, let the magic of the present moment fill you up. Love this moment as much as you possibly can because someday, this moment will be a memory too.

soak it all in

Soak it all in. The life around you. The abundance. The beauty. The light. The magic. The air. The breeze. The sounds of the earth. The rising sun. The phases of the moon. *Soak it all in.* Allow yourself to truly and deeply experience everything this life has for you.

Soak it all in. The harder things too. The darkness. The pain. The hurts. Let yourself feel them deeply. And then learn to let them go. By knowing the dark, you will know true light. By feeling the pain, you will know true joy.

Soak it all in. Feel it all and let it into your heart. Sing. Dance. Run free. Play. Wonder. Dream. Laugh. Cry. Ask questions. Ponder ideas. Wish. Try. *Love.*

The greatest treasures of life can be found right around you if you open your heart wide to all of the life that is already there for you.

deserving

It is not too good to be true,
you deserve this.
You earned this.
You worked so hard for this.

Welcome the good.
Invite it into your heart.
Celebrate your work.
Celebrate all that you've done.
Celebrate all that you poured into.

Do not brush it off.
Do not discredit yourself.
You earned this.

You deserve this good.
Be proud of yourself.
Celebrate all that you've done.

You are worthy of all of the good.

welcome the good

There is so much good meant just for *you*. There is more joy and abundance and love than you could ever imagine out in the world for you. So welcome the good into your life. Accept all of the good and abundance that is meant for you with gratitude and love. Know that you are deserving of it. When good things happen, welcome them into your heart with thankfulness. Allow the joy around you into your spirit. Open your heart to the love that is there for you. Open your mind to the answers trying to find you. Stay open to receiving all of the good around you, because it is trying to find you too.

being okay

In those moments when you say that you are okay when you really aren't, remember that it really is okay to not be okay. It is *human* to not be okay. It is okay to feel down. It is okay to feel sad or hurt or frustrated or upset... But what is *not* okay is ignoring those feelings when you are not okay. It is not okay to lie to yourself about how you are feeling. If you are feeling down, do not ignore it or shove it aside... The only way to resolve these feelings is to accept them and let yourself feel them. Ask yourself why you are feeling that way. Is it something that is easy to resolve or something deeper? Be kind to yourself. Give yourself time to process what needs to be processed. Some wounds cut deeper than we realize and won't heal overnight. And some wounds continue to resurface again and again until they are truly healed.

Remind yourself that whatever you are feeling truly is okay. Be kind to yourself. Give yourself grace. Ask yourself what would help you feel a little better. What little or big things could you do *right now* to move forward back to feeling good again? What things can you let go of *right now*? The way towards feeling okay again is acknowledging the moments when you aren't, and learning how to let those feelings in and then, *let those feelings out*.

my hope for you

May this new day hold the answers to the questions you have been holding onto for so long. May this day bring you a feeling of deep peace that you have not felt for a long time. May this day allow you to find space in your heart to let go and forgive all of the things and people that need to be forgiven (*including yourself*). May this day bring unexpected and wonderful new joys. May the sun peek through the clouds to greet you and fill you with its warmth. May this day remind you that life is a beautiful gift and that it is worth living deeply, loving always, and cherishing every single day.

step up first

Sometimes you will have to go first. You might have to be the first one of your friends to step into your potential. You might have to be the first one in your family to break a harmful generational pattern. You might have to be the first one in your work to say no to tolerating abuse. You might have to be the first one in the room who is kind. You might have to be the one to step up first.

So step up first. Be the one who brings change. Be the first one to hold your boundaries firm. Be the first one to forgive. Be the first one to step into your true potential. *Be the first one.* Someone has to do it first, so why not you? Do not wait for someone to give you permission to do what is right for you. Do not wait for someone else to step up first. Step up despite those who want to keep you down. Step up regardless of who remains with you as you expand and grow. Whenever you feel the pull, whenever you need to expand, whenever you just know it's time, do not be afraid to step up first.

a brighter lens

Whatever you look for in this world,
you will find.

Joy.
Love.
Purpose.
Passion.
Courage.
Change.
Opportunity.
Peace.
Kindness.
Possibility.
Sorrow.
Pain.
Setbacks.
Regrets.
Impossibility.

Every now and again,
make sure to check in on the lens
that you are using.
Maybe you need to dust it off or
switch it out for a brighter one,
but make sure you are seeking what you hope to find.

simplifying

Less overthinking and more living.
Less overanalyzing and more appreciating.
Less wondering and more enjoying.
Less worrying and more being.
Less needing and more thanking.
Less controlling and more letting be.
Maybe it really is simpler than we realize.

making room for joy

You are meant for so much joy. The joy that makes you forget about time altogether. The joy that makes you want more moments to last forever. The joy that makes you fall in love with life. The joy that makes your cheeks ache from smiling for so long. The joy that lights a fire in your soul… You are not meant to walk through life numb to the world around you. You are not meant to hold onto all of the hurts from your past— they take up too much space in your heart. My beautiful friend, your heart is meant to light up with joy. Not every day will have fireworks and not every day can be the best day of your life, but every day does hold joy for you. Every single one. And it is up to *you* to make room for it.

III. Passion

your gifts

You have more beautiful, unique gifts than you know. Things that you just do normally that other people wish that they could do. The way you are brave. The way you take on every new challenge. The way you are kind and empathetic towards everyone. The way you care about those around you. The way you see the world like no one else… Your gifts are sacred. What you offer the world, *no one else can*. Be proud of your unique gifts. Celebrate your talents. Share them with the world.

no one does it like you

Make your beautiful art.
No one creates it like you.
Give your unique love.
No one shares it like you.
Tackle the tough challenges.
No one overcomes them like you.
Do not quiet down your sound because
you think that it does not belong in the music of life.
This world would not be what it is
without your voice, without your gifts.
Your impact goes far beyond what you will ever know.
So sing. Love. Create. Make. Give. *Celebrate your gifts.*

just past the fear

Something magical happens when you feel the fear, *lean into it,* and move bravely, boldly forward anyway. I imagine it is like the feeling a bird must have jumping off a steep ledge— a brief moment of enormous, consuming fear, jumping anyway, and then— *taking flight. Soaring across the skies.* Following a big dream, jumping into something new, running that big race, creating that huge project, telling someone you love them for the first time, going outside of your comfort zone— all of these are like that... There is a lot of fear in the unknown, and we are wired to have reservations of jumping into the unknown. But there is a moment just beyond the fear. A moment of magic. A moment of letting in the fear, feeling it, and then *turning the fear into faith.* Turning the fear of falling into the faith of flying. *That* is the moment of magic. Leaning into the fear and transforming it into faith, jumping, and then— *soaring.*

playing it safe

The thing about playing it safe is that the more often you do, the harder it becomes to step out of your comfort zone. And the harder it becomes to step out of your comfort zone, the more you will want to stay where it is safe and predictable. And as the cycle continues, it strengthens itself. So make sure every now and again, you *break the cycle* and step away from your comfort zone to try something brand new. You are not meant to live your whole life safely inside of your comfort zone anyway. You are not meant to live the same way every day, every week, every year. You are not meant to play it safe in every single decision you make. There is a certain practicality and some risks are not worth taking, but more often than not, magic is to be found just beyond the walls of your comfort zone. New, deeper joy is to be found just beyond what you have always known. New experiences that you will wonder how you ever lived without. People that you will love and people that will love you. Places that will become your favorite spot to visit in your free time. Experiences that will make you grow and expand in ways you could have never imagined. Play it safe when you must, but when your heart begs for more, *take the leap*.

nothing is wasted

Not all plans work out. And not all plans *need* to work out. Sometimes, things fall through because something else requires more attention and energy. Sometimes, things get postponed enough times that they end up being canceled. Sometimes, things just do not work out even when you gave it everything you had. But nothing— *and I mean nothing*— is ever wasted. The time spent on a project that never came to fruition gave incredible experience and growth that will make the next project that much easier. The job you poured into before completely changing careers gave you a deeper understanding of yourself. Learning what you love is important, but so is learning what you *don't* love. Everything you pour yourself into gives you experience, growth, and a deeper understanding of yourself— *nothing* is ever wasted.

soul garden

You have all you will ever need within you already. You have the soil, the seeds, the water, the light. You have *everything* you need to become all that you are seeking.

Sow the seeds you would like to see grow in the garden of your soul. If you would like your life to hold more joy, plant more seeds of joy: celebrate more things that are in your life— whether people or trees or things. Celebrate more moments, celebrate the little things and the big things more. If you would like your life to hold more peace, plant more seeds of peace: create moments of stillness right were you are. Look to nature and her peaceful rhythms and remember that you can feel the same peace. If you would like your life to hold more love, plant more seeds of love: be loving. Spread kindness. Give more hugs. Ask more people how they really are. If you would like more fulfillment, plant more seeds of fulfillment: seek out more activities that light a fire in you. Help others, give your time and energy to help change someone's life.

Whatever it is you are looking for, always know that you hold the seeds and the power for them to grow.

guiding light

Trust your intuition. Trust the pulls you feel towards people and jobs and experiences. Your intuition is your guiding light. *Let it guide you.* Whenever you are making a big decision or choosing a path to take, sit with yourself first. Make space away from the noise of others and the world to listen to what your intuition is telling you. The answers will come to you if you make space to listen for them. So, make space. Let your intuition guide you. It is always guiding you home to yourself.

inner wisdom

There is time for seeking wisdom from others, but there is also time for quieting down the outside world and listening to your own inner wisdom. You hold many more answers than you may realize. Your gut feelings and heart inklings mean something. Trust them. Learn to listen to your intuition. Learn to trust the feelings inside of you about the situations and people around you. Often times, your heart and intuition know before your mind can process those feelings with logic. Listen to it. Trust your inner wisdom. You already hold all of the answers you are looking for.

to live passionately

To live passionately is to nourish the flame within your beating heart. To live passionately is to choose to be excited about what you are creating, what you are giving, what you are working towards each day.

And sometimes we think that passion will come to us. We think that if we wait for it, it will come and fuel *us*. But the exact opposite is true— passion *follows* action. *We* fuel our passion by getting up, showing up, and giving every last drop we have.

If you work on something you love, your passion will grow. If you wait for passion to find you, you will be waiting your whole life.

You have to *choose* to live passionately. You have to choose to nourish the fire within you and do things that fuel your spark for life. You have to choose to be passionate about the life you are living— and if you cannot find any passion for the days you are moving through, it might be time to change things so that you can find passion for your daily life.

To live passionately is to live each day fully and entirely. It is laying your head on the pillow completely exhausted and satisfied that you didn't leave any moment of the day un-lived. To live passionately is to let your fire burn strong and to continually feed its flames. It is to live each day fully *alive*.

IV. Love

falling in love with being alive

Love the ordinary things like they are extraordinary. Love the way your bed feels in the morning— its warmth and coziness. Fall in love with the sounds outside your window— whether it is the hum of cars hustling by or the stillness of the trees. Love the way your feet crunch into the fresh snow in early winter and love the way the morning dew smells in early spring. Love the way that the seasons change and love the ways that you change. Love the way the moon goes through phases and how the sun moves. Find a way to love Mondays because they are 14 percent of your whole life and that 14 percent deserves to be loved too. Find a way to love the long winters and the summer storms and all of the days in between. *Find reasons to love it all* because *it is all a part of life*. A part of *your* life. And my beautiful friend, you deserve a life that you *love*.

in all that you do

In all that you do, may you do it with love.
May you love the people you spend your time with,
the places you go,
the ways you spend your time,
the experiences you try,
and all of the precious moments given to you.
May you love it all entirely
and *never be afraid to show it.*
May you find new ways
to fall in love with your life
over and over and over again.

you do not need to do it alone

You do not need to do it alone. You do not need to carry the weight all by yourself. You do not need to prove that you are strong enough to do it alone. You do not need to prove it to yourself or to anyone else… Asking for support does not make you weak. Asking for advice or even just a hug on a hard day does not mean you could not do it… You *can* do anything by yourself— you are strong and smart and capable enough— but you do not need to. You have people around you who *want* to be there for you. You have beautiful souls around you that love being by your side. You have people who would rather fight by your side than see you fight alone. We are so much stronger together. The weight is lighter, the pain is more bearable. There are times for working by yourself, but there are times for leaning into your support, too. Allow yourself to lean into your team because it is what makes you strong.

in all forms

To love the sky is to love it in all of its forms. To love the sky is to love its pastel sunrises, misty mornings, cloudless days full of sun, crescent moon nights. Its raging August storms, its clouded nights, its grey overcast days. To love the sky is to love it in all of its forms. And loving people is like that too… To love someone is to love them on both the days it is easy and the days that it is hard. To love someone is to love their sunrises and beautiful days and their stormy days too. To love someone is to love them entirely, *in all forms.*

forgive often

Allow yourself to forgive often. Allow yourself to forgive others and yourself too. Forgive others for their wrongdoings or mistakes. Forgive others for hurting you. Forgiveness does not mean that what they did was justified or right, and it does not mean that you need to keep them in your life. You can have boundaries for who you are allowing in your life while simultaneously forgiving those who do not hold a place in your life anymore. Forgiving them means that you are letting go of the weight of their actions from the past.

Make sure you forgive yourself too. You do not need to be so hard on yourself and beat yourself up for things you regret. Forgive yourself for your mistakes and the times when you treated others unkindly or unfairly. Forgive yourself for the things from your past that you are still carrying with you today. When you forgive, you make space in your heart for peace *today*. When you hold onto grudges or past mistakes, you let go of today's peace to hold yesterday's weight. Forgive often and make room in your heart for peace today.

loving you

There are so many reasons to love you.
So take the time to love you.
Take the time to love your eyes and your smile.
Your body and your heart.
Your fingers, your stomach.
Your mind, your soul.
Take the time to love you.
Your growth. Your progress.
Your successes and your failures.
Take the time to love all of these things
because they are the very things that
make you so uniquely you.
Take the time to love you—
all of you.
You are worthy of your own love.

on loving yourself

Choose to love yourself entirely. Choose to embrace your flaws and forgive your mistakes. Choose to embrace yourself for all that you are.

Loving yourself is about accepting yourself. It's fighting for yourself and believing in yourself. It's picking yourself back up after you fall because you know that you are worthy of standing tall again. Loving yourself is cherishing who you are and nurturing your body and spirit. It is acknowledging yourself and embracing yourself for who you truly are. It is treating yourself kindly. It is in the way you think and talk about yourself. It is in the way you fill up your cup.

Before all else, you must nurture the relationship you have with yourself because it is the foundation for the relationship you have with the people and world around you. If you are constantly hard on yourself, it will feel like the world is constantly hard on you. If you are constantly loving yourself, the world will love you too. *How you treat yourself is how you allow the world to treat you.* So be kind to yourself. Love yourself, my beautiful friend. You are worthy of your love.

on loving beautiful things

Beautiful things do not need to be understood in order to be loved. You do not need to understand how mountains were formed to stand in front of one and stare in awe at its great size. You do not need to understand why the ocean has waves to find peace in their rhythms. You do not need to understand why life is the way it is in order to love it. And each day does not need to be understood to be loved either... You can have uncertainty or lack clarity while still loving the day. You can be in between jobs or places or people and still love your days anyways. Because in times of uncertainty— in the time of in-between's— the *very best thing* you can do is to love the present moment anyways. To live each day with a loving and open heart. To celebrate yourself and others and good things. To keep a grateful and light heart... Because a day that is lived in love is a day well-lived.

V. Growth

the practice of growing slowly

Everything you are growing towards is growing towards you too. Your dreams are not rushing away from you. Your plans are not moving away from you— they do not need to be perfectly laid out or achieved right this moment... Take your time with your growth. Forcing growth leads to stress, anxiety, and overwhelm. Intentional and steady growth leads to joy, fulfillment, and a beautiful bloom. There is a difference between trying to force something that is just not possible at this stage and pushing yourself to grow into your next level. Only you will know where the line is for *you*. Take your time with your growth. Let yourself take the small steps. Know that a small step is always, *always* better than no step at all. A ten minute walk is better than no walk at all. A few pages of reading is better than none at all. Thirty seconds of intentional breathing is better than zero. The small steps you take add up faster than you realize. So let yourself grow slowly. Let your bloom take its time. You are growing. You are on your way. And I promise that you'll get there before you know.

un-rushed

Growth is beautiful when it is not rushed—
when it is nurtured and loved and cared for
the entire way from seed to bloom.

You cannot rush your own becoming.
You cannot rush yourself into a beautiful growth.
You must pour into your growth
little by little.
One moment at a time.
One day at a time.
Water yourself with patience and trust.
Nourish yourself with kindness and love.
Let the seeds you plant unfold in their own time.

growth beneath the surface

You do not always see the progress you are making because a lot of the progress cannot be seen. A lot of it happens internally, deep beneath the surface. *That* is why you must trust yourself and the work you are putting in, my beautiful friend. *That* is why you keep going even when you do not see the change yet.

As you work on becoming a better version of yourself, your mind is hard at work changing and expanding. Your body is getting stronger within before you will see it on the outside. The healing you are doing is happening deeply— you may not realize it or feel it, but every moment you commit to your healing you are taking a step towards your growth. It takes time to realize how much you are growing, and it takes patience to see your blooms. Keep trust in the process. Keep working on yourself. And know that even when you cannot see it yet, you are growing beneath the surface.

always choose to grow

There is always a choice. To go or to stay. To grow or to remain. To jump or to stay on the ground. To try again or to give up. *There is always a choice.* Choose to grow. Choose to learn. Choose to release your ego and learn from your shortcomings, your mistakes, and your faults. Choose to continue becoming the best version of yourself. Know that the blessings, the lessons, and the teachings are all *for* you. Not to hurt you, not to make you feel guilt or shame or hurt. But to teach you how to rise. To teach you how to heal. To teach you how to love and find joy. Nothing is against you. The things happening to you all have blessings and lessons in them, and it is up to you to see them. Let the lessons teach you and keep you humble. Learn from them and continue forward. Let the blessings remind you of the magic of life. Savor them and let them fill your heart. Know that everything happening to you can help you grow if you let it. My beautiful friend, choose to grow every time.

take the pressure off

It is time to take the pressure off of yourself, my beautiful friend. It is time to let go of the pressure from others to perform, to fit into a mold, to be a certain way. It is time to let go of the pressure to grow faster... *Take your time. Take off the pressure.* There is a balance in setting goals and working towards growth, and the balance should not feel like a clock ticking quickly towards zero. It should not feel like an impossible deadline that you have to bend and break yourself in order to get there. Growth should not feel rushed or forced. Growth happens *naturally*. Everything in our world grows in its own time, it is the nature of life. So when your growth feels forced, when it feels rushed, when it feels like the pressure of the world is coming down on you, take that pressure off of yourself. Set it down. Let it go. Toss it away. Let yourself grow without the clock. Let yourself grow in all of the ways that *you* are meant to grow, in the time that you are meant to take.

the truth

The truth is that the little choices you make each day often will change your life *exponentially* more than any big choice you make. The way you change your life is by changing what you do on your normal, typical days. The way you start your mornings. The way you show yourself love and the way you show others love. How you handle problems and disruptions and conflicts. What you do in the face of fear. How much you look for joy. How you feed your mind, body, and spirit. How much you fill up your cup and how much you pour. What you do in your evenings… You change your life by changing the little things… You change your life one moment at a time. You change your life one *choice*— to be a little better, a little kinder, a little braver— at a time.

who you can become

There is no limit to who you can become— to who you can grow into. Growth is so much more about the *journey* of becoming and less about reaching the destination. Though there are countless beautiful milestones along the way, true growth is about *becoming* the person who can do those things more than it is about actually doing those things... It is about becoming the person who believes in yourself and all that you can accomplish. It is about becoming the person who is determined and strong and follows through. It is about becoming the greatest version of who *you* want to be, so that you can do everything you dream of doing.

never stop dreaming

Keep dreaming. Don't wait to think of or plan new ideas. Don't wait until you have enough time or money or courage. Don't wait for others to say it is okay to dream. *Dream.* Dream up new adventures. Dream up new things that light fireworks in your soul. Dream up dreams for no purpose apart from allowing your soul the space to sing. My beautiful friend, dream so wildly big. Dream of what you want to do with your one wild and beautiful and precious life. Oh my beautiful friend, dream and do not ever stop. Set your soul free. Release any limits. Dreaming big even if you don't make it all the way will get you a lot closer to your dream life than dreaming small ever will. Keep dreaming and keep taking steps towards bringing them to life. You have one precious life to dream up and live your most beautiful life. Don't be afraid to make it entirely, beautifully *yours*.

trust yourself

Trust yourself. Trust your growth. Trust your intuition. Trust your strength. Trust your abilities. Trust your journey. Trust that the things you are going through are supporting your becoming. Trust that you will find the people meant for you. Really, *truly* trust yourself, my beautiful friend. Trust yourself so that it does not matter what others say or what obstacles come your way— you will keep forging on and believing in your path. Trust yourself and your journey so much that you are so focused on forward that it really doesn't matter what distractions happen around you. Remain strong and steady in yourself. You've got this. You really truly do. You are doing beyond great. Whether others recognize it or not, *you. are. doing. great.* So keep being you, keep trusting yourself. You are on your way.

beyond the struggle

No matter what struggle you are facing, there is something beautiful beyond this. Something wonderful. Something that will make all of this worth it. Something that will make this make sense. You are meant to overcome, to grow, and to flourish through this. No struggle can keep you from your ever expanding growth and becoming.

No path worth walking comes easy because the difficulties are what give you the opportunity to grow. Difficulties make you look at yourself— *really* look at yourself— and make you question whether you are going to grow through it or hide from it. And every time you choose growth, you are choosing to see the light on the other side. *So choose growth.* Choose to find the beauty in the fractured seed. Choose to see the beauty in the waiting. Choose to see the light in the aching... Because as soon as you flip the compass inside of you towards the light, you will never be stuck in the dark again.

be kind to yourself

You cannot be so hard on yourself, I mean it. You cannot keep tearing yourself down for your mistakes or failures and expect yourself to rise up. The more you beat up on yourself while you are going through hard times, the harder it will be on you. The more you give yourself love and grace and the more you lift yourself, the easier it will be to stand back up. The more you trust in your ability to rise, the easier it will be to rise up and continue ahead. Beating up on yourself for your mistakes is like kicking yourself when you are *already* down. It does not help. It does not do *any* good. It does not encourage you or make you feel like getting up— it keeps you down. So stop. Stop beating up on yourself. Practice loving yourself harder when you're down. Practice lifting yourself up and being kind to yourself. Remind yourself that when you make mistakes, it means that you are stretching and growing, and that is *good*. You won't be perfect on your first try and you do not need to be. Let yourself be awful on your first try. Let yourself mess up without beating yourself up for it. Let yourself learn and grow without judging yourself so harshly. Love yourself. Be kind to yourself. You are growing beautifully.

infinite possibilities

There are infinite possibilities for you and your life. *Infinite*. So you have to start believing that you can bring that magic to life. You have to start doing all of the things that you dream of doing. Because you can. Because it's all possible. Because all that it takes to change your life is to change a single thought about what you believe is possible. First, one thought of something that you believe is possible for yourself. Then, another. Then, you begin to act on those thoughts. You start doing those things you've always wanted to do. And you realize that you really can do more than you thought. *That* is how you change your life. By deciding. And doing. One decision— one moment— at a time.

beautiful, unexpected treasures

Let life surprise you.
Let life take you on journeys that
you never thought to take.
Let life lead you to unexpected places with
unexpected people and unexpected experiences
that open your eyes and heart.

Some plans won't go the way you intend.
Some paths won't work out and
some doors will close.
And that's okay.
Not all plans need to work out.
Not all doors are meant to open for you.
Sometimes life needs to guide you
towards new places because
you can't find the unexpected treasures on your own.
So when plans fall through,
when things don't go the way that
you thought they would,
surrender.

Let life guide you towards all of its
beautiful, unexpected treasures
that are meant just for *you*.

pursue

Pursue more of the things that light a spark in your soul.
More of the things that make you feel whole.
More of the things that make you feel peace.
More of the things that are true to *you*.

honor your dreams

Do you honor your dreams? Do you own up to them? Do you trust yourself and your abilities to bring them to life? My beautiful friend, it is time to *own up to your dreams*. To honor them. To be honest with yourself. Are there changes in your life that you have been wanting to make for a long time but just haven't found the means or the time? Are you truly becoming the person you have always wanted to become? Or are you holding yourself back in some way?

It takes courage and honesty to look at yourself, and I mean to really truly look at yourself and the person you are becoming. But when you do— when you take a real good look at yourself and your life— you won't be able to hide from yourself or your dreams anymore. And it isn't easy because when you stop hiding from yourself and your intuitions, you'll realize that you cannot blame anyone else, and that your life is in your hands. And that is a scary thought, but it's freeing too.

You'll no longer accept less than what you deserve. You'll no longer settle for things when you know you are meant for more. You won't be able to hide from your dreams anymore because they'll be staring right back at you. *This* is your sign. *This* is your call to do something about it. To step into your courage and to be intentional about your life.

time to reflect

Take time to reflect. Take time to look back on how far you have come and how much you have grown. I mean it, my beautiful friend, when was the last time you really, *really* took a moment to celebrate just how far you've come?

Every now and again, take a break from charging forward to pause and be proud of all of the progress you have made. And when you finish something big, really, *truly* take the time to celebrate the big thing you just completed. Whatever it is. Whether or not it is big to others. If it is big to you, *celebrate it.* Too often, we charge right into the next thing without absorbing and reflecting on what we just finished. Sometimes we climb up an entire mountain, spending months or years on the climb, only to get to the top and quickly see and plan the next one we hope to climb, which is perfectly human... But what we don't always realize is that a lot of growth happens when we take the time to absorb all that we did. So take the time to reflect on the lessons you learned and the strength you gained throughout your trials. Take the time to realize your growth. Let it sink in. Absorb it. Let yourself be proud. *Let yourself celebrate.* There will always be another mountain to climb, but before you pack up and go, make sure you celebrate this one.

patience in the waiting

It isn't always easy to see a season of waiting as a blessing. It may feel like nothing is moving, nothing is happening, or you aren't making any progress. But the truth is that these seasons of waiting are when the *most* growth is happening. It is when the growth is happening *underneath* the surface. During the times of waiting, keep watering the seeds and trusting that they will soon sprout and bloom. Keep letting the seeds do their work and stay patient. Let the season of waiting be not about waiting for the bloom, but rather, a season of enjoying all that is already blooming around you. A season of loving the blessings around you now. A season of celebrating how much it took to get you *here*. Keep watering your seeds and working on yourself. Know that you are growing deep beneath the surface and keep celebrating all the blooms around you.

in the seasons of waiting

There is only one good way to wait— and that is by celebrating all that you hold already. There are so many things you hold now that you once wished so badly for. There are so many blessings around you that you once only dreamed of having. So when you are in a season of waiting, let it be a season of celebrating instead. A season of counting your blessings. There is so much ahead of you that is on its way to you— beautiful things. Beautiful dreams. Wonderful moments and boundless love. And sometimes they take their time to arrive to you. So in that in-between time, *celebrate*. Celebrate the blessings that surround you. There is so much ahead for you, but there is also so much right now for you.

taking a leap

Sometimes you just have to
take the leap.
Of faith.
Of trust.
Of hope.
Of belief…

Sometimes you just have to
trust your inner voice
regardless of what others say.
Sometimes you just have to
trust that it is leading you
in the right direction
towards the right people,
the right places, the right jobs,
and the right experiences.

Because a single leap
just might be
the *very* thing that changes
everything.

VI. Expression

true authenticity

You are worthy of true authenticity. You are worthy of letting your guard down and letting yourself be seen for all that you are— both the things you love about yourself and the things that you don't. You do not need to hide any of it, my beautiful friend. Not your beauty and not your scars. You do not need to cover up any part of you… You are worthy of showing your authentic self to world.

Nikki Banas

the first spring blooms

Like the first tulips
of early spring do not hesitate to
push through the cold, hard ground
to make their own space under the golden sun,

do not hesitate to make room for yourself too.

boldly, beautifully, wonderfully you

There will always be people who will find a reason to dislike you. You will be too much for some and too little for others. Some people need to find flaws in others to find confidence in themselves. Some people do not want you to show your true self because they aren't ready to show their true self yet. Some people just might be having a bad day and pour it onto you... So please, *please*, stop bending and breaking yourself into someone that you think they will like. Stop trying to change your true nature and your true colors to be more like theirs. Do not spend any more energy trying to fit into a crowd you were never meant to walk with... You are meant to be *you*. You are meant to be boldly, beautifully, wonderfully, spectacularly, authentically *you*. Do not let anyone keep you from setting your spirit free. Do not be afraid to speak up first. Do not be afraid to dance to the music of your soul. Set yourself free from other's expectations. You are here to live the life that *you* dream of living.

your magic

Your magic comes from being you.
Not from trying to be like anyone else—
Not from trying to be how you think you 'should' be—
but from simply, being *you*.

Your magic comes from letting yourself be seen exactly
as you are. Your magic comes when you say what you
mean and be who you want to be. It comes from
choosing the jobs you love and spending time with the
people you love. It comes from letting go of all those who
drain your spirit and don't see your shine. Your magic
comes when you stop trying to prove that you deserve to
be here, and when you start just fully and entirely, *being
here*. Your magic comes when you realize there is no
competition or race, nor has there *ever* been. It has
always been about simply being yourself, moving at your
own pace, and letting your magic shine.

your ocean soul

Breathtaking ocean soul, do not shy away from your stunning depths. Allow yourself to plunge. To dive into yourself. To get to know your endless waters and your unique waves. Allow yourself to learn how to sail your seas and navigate through your storms. To learn how to bring peace to your waters and to celebrate your magnificent colors. Breathtaking ocean soul, do not shy away from your stunning depths. Plunge into them and learn to love the seas within.

you are allowed to be you

You are allowed to be loud.
You are allowed to be soft.
You are allowed to use your voice.
You are allowed to take up space.
You are allowed to take off any masks you wear and let your authentic self be seen just as you are.
You are allowed to say what you mean.
You are allowed to do what you dream.
You are allowed to change your mind.

You are allowed to be so wonderfully you, that the world has no other choice, than to be in wonder at just how beautiful the true you is.

being courageous

Maybe being courageous is not about one grand act or a single big moment. Maybe being brave doesn't come loudly. Maybe it's quiet sometimes. Softer. Gentler. Maybe being courageous is made from taking smaller steps or even slower steps in the right direction.

Maybe courage is found in the little choices you make each day. Like taking a small step out of your comfort zone— whether by saying a new hello or allowing yourself to be a beginner in trying something new. Standing up for yourself or standing up for someone else. Putting yourself out there…

Maybe courage isn't reserved for just the big, grand moments of passion and intensity— but for all of the little moments in between, too.

creation

Create without inhibition. Dance without fear. Write without worry. Move freely. Create what feels good to create. Make the things that you want to make. Humans are creators. We have been throughout our *entire* history. We make. We create. We build. We cook. We bake. We turn ideas into real things. We turn a few ingredients or supplies into stunning things. It is in our blood. There is no wrong way to make your art. There is only you, making your art. We do not make things because we can. We make them because we are *made* to make things. It does not matter what your final product looks like or if anyone else likes it. Create for *you*. Create because the art in you is just itching to get out of your mind and into the world. Create because you can. Create to express yourself. There is no one like you… No one sees it like you do, no one feels it all like you do. And that is why we need what only *you* can create.

time alone

Do not be afraid to spend time alone. Spend time getting to know who you are without the influence of all of those around you. Spend time learning how to rely on yourself for your happiness and your comfort. Spend time finding what really brings you fulfillment and peace, and what things don't. Spend time figuring out what things stress you out and overwhelm you, and figuring out how to return back to calm.

Do not be afraid to spend time alone. To spend time discovering and deciding who you want to be without the pressure of others. To truly meet yourself and love yourself. To learn how to be there for yourself and take care of yourself when others aren't around to help you.

You will find clarity alone. You will find answers and new dreams. You will have the space to truly understand your feelings and thoughts. You will find the space to heal yourself and discover your process. The more you become comfortable spending time with yourself, the more you will find peace and calm for your mind, heart, and spirit.

belonging

You belong. You have a place here. You are a divine and sacred part of our world. Your impact goes further than you could ever know. Even if you feel different, even if you feel like you are out of place, there is space here just for you. You belong here.

And in the times that you feel most out of place, may you find your way into a forest or out to the ocean and witness all of the ways the earth makes room for every tree, every wave, every ladybug, and every daisy. There is space for every plant and every stream, every animal and every passing cloud.

And alongside it all, *there is space meant just for you, too.*

become completely undone

Before you come alive in your full expression, you must become completely undone. Like how the seed breaks its shell open before it can grow and bloom... You have to take a good look at yourself. Not a quick glance, but a real and raw moment of asking yourself who you are and who you want to be. You have to face yourself and be truly vulnerable and honest with yourself. You have to take off all of the fronts you wear for the world and remind yourself of who you are underneath it all.

Who are you? What do you want? What do you *really* want? Who do you *really* want to be? Are you living the life you want to be living? If there was no pressure to do or be a certain way, who would you decide to be? If you allowed your spirit to be completely free, what would you do?

Break open your shell and allow yourself to become completely undone. And then, my beautiful friend, *set yourself free.*

never stuck

Sometimes we forget that we are not stuck. Whether we have been living in the same patterns for years or believing the same things our whole lives, sometimes we forget that it is perfectly human to change your mind as you learn and grow more.

You are allowed to change up everything or nothing at all. You are allowed to change your belief system because you learned new things and it changed your perception. You are allowed to change up what you are doing if you are exhausted of moving through the same routine day in and day out. You are allowed to change things up and move around. You are allowed to move into something new if you feel a nudge of wanting something different.

Change can be as little or as drastic as you would like it to be. And of course others will not always be on board or understand, but do not let anyone keep you from those nudges inside of your heart. Never let others keep you from *you*. Allow yourself to change with the movements in your heart— your heart is always guiding you home to yourself.

your power

Never let yourself feel powerless. Remember that you *always* have power, my beautiful friend. You are never stuck. You have the power to bring change to your mind, to your career, your hobbies, your home, your world, and your relationships. You are *never* powerless. Even if it feels like you are stuck someplace, you hold the power to change things. You can bring change to your inner world— which in time, will change your entire world outside too. You can start something new. You can talk to someone new or read a new book to open your perspective. You can visit someplace new—whether a new spot in your city or another country entirely. You have the power to be the change you want. Whenever you want or need, my beautiful friend, do not be afraid to use your power and bring change into your life.

all that shines within you

You have so many beautiful
pieces and layers and intricacies that
make you so wildly and wonderfully *you*.
Dive into yourself.
Plunge into your being.
Meet yourself.
Explore your depths.
Express yourself fully.
Let your truest self shine out into the world.

VII. Peace

a pause

Soften your shoulders.
Fill your lungs (with as much air as you possibly can)
Reach your arms up high and feel the stretch.
Welcome peace into your heart.
Breathe in.
Exhale any tension.
Soak in the world around you. *Really look.*
Notice something you have never noticed before.
Release all that is heavy.

peace is a practice

Like all things, peace is a practice. The practice of letting go and letting be. The practice of allowing thoughts to pass. The practice of allowing others to be others and allowing yourself to be yourself. The practice of forgiveness. The practice of release. The practice of patience. The practice of surrender. The practice of seeing that peace *already* resides within and around you and letting it fill your heart and spirit.

worthy of peace

You, my beautiful friend, are worthy of peace. You are worthy of healing your wounds and moving forward in peace. You are worthy of the time that it takes to heal those wounds. You are worthy of the rest and the soul work it takes to truly meet and accept yourself. You are worthy of nourishing your world within— the way you talk to yourself, the way you respond to conflict, the way that you take on each new day. You are worthy of feeling peace, no matter what storms you have seen and endured. You are worthy of letting peace into your heart and soul.

living peacefully

To live in peace is to live each day with no weight of yesterday nor tomorrow. It is to live each moment without a thought of the days behind or the days ahead of you. It is realizing that everything you need is here for you in this moment already... To live in peace is to live each moment as it comes, with full presentness and aliveness.

light & dark

There will always be light and dark. Yin and yang. Push and pull, ebb and flow. Days of questions and days of answers. Seasons of winter and seasons of summer. Times of growth and times of rest. Moments of joy and moments of sadness... Peace is knowing that all of these things exist *together*, and that that is the nature of life. And peace is knowing that nothing is permanent— that a season of blooming cannot last forever but neither will a season of darkness. Peace is found not in trying to hold onto only the good times, but in embracing *all* times. Peace is found in accepting and embracing the nature of life.

processing emotions

There will always be sadness and anger, hurt and heartaches, disappointments and frustrations. The way towards peace is never by avoiding theses feelings. And it is never by sealing these emotions inside without a way to let them out. Peace is found in learning what your mind and soul need to do to process these emotions in a healthy way. Peace is found in learning how to let out your angers and hurts in a way that brings you back to feeling light and free again. Peace is found in accepting that life will bring every emotion and that it is up to *you* how you want to ride with them. You can ignore them as long as you can— but they will fester and grow until one day you have no choice but to release them. You can fight them— but you will never find peace through fighting with yourself and the emotions you are feeling. So you must learn how to let yourself feel them fully *and* learn how to let them go to return to your peace.

little reminders

Sometimes it really is the simple reminders that we need the most.

Breathe. Smile. It will be okay. You are okay. You are enough. You matter. You are doing better than you think. Bad days happen. Better days are always ahead. Keep going. Keep trying. Just one step at a time. Know your worth *(priceless)*. Do not settle. Be grateful for what you're going through. Be kind to yourself. Be a light to others too. Give yourself time. Give others time.

Sometimes it really is the simple reminders that we need the most.

take your time

Take your time everywhere you go. Release the moments of later and the moments of yesterday, and fill this moment of here and now with peace. There is no need to rush through the day or *get through* another day. So many wonderful things are found in stillness and slowness. When you slow down as you are eating, you can taste every aspect and flavor of your meal so much more. When you slow down as you are walking, you can see so much more of the world you are walking through... Take your time. Savor more. Live *deeply*.

on facing change

Allow yourself to move like the ocean waves through change. Life is meant to be lived— it does not need to be fully understood or figured out to be enjoyed. So allow yourself to live it fully and deeply, even when you do not understand it all— *especially* when you do not understand it all... Trust that you are on your divine path, and that this moment is a stepping stone in your path towards your greatest self. Ride the waves as they come, just one at a time. Embrace each wave with love, openness, and grace for all that it brings you.

beyond the horizon

You do not need to be able to see
beyond the horizon
to find joy in these shores.

moving with the winds

There is a lot of strength in flexibility. In being able to bend and move with the wind instead of fighting against it. In being able to ride the waves and float with the currents instead of fighting their pulls. So allow yourself to move with the winds and the currents of your life. Know that nothing stays the same; life is always changing, life is always in motion. If you are being pulled in a new direction, go with it. Ride it. Move with it. If you are facing new depths of emotion that you haven't before, feel them. Let yourself explore the depths of your heart. When you allow yourself to move with change instead of fighting against it, you will discover your greatest strength. When you realize you do not need to control the waves— nor the winds— and that your job is simply to make the most of the ride, my beautiful friend, you will be free.

surrendering

There is so much freedom in
surrendering,
letting go,
and releasing
all that is not yours to hold.

What if, just for today, you welcomed in slowness?

What if, just for today, you took it all just a little bit slower?

What if, just for today, you *really* took your time drinking your coffee? What if you really took your time making it and pouring it into your mug? What if you really took your time allowing its aroma to fill your senses before you took that first sip?

What if, just for today, you let yourself have moments of nothing? Moments to simply be. Moments to sit and look around at your world and breathe.

What if, just for today, you did not rush yourself so much? What if you allowed yourself to really enjoy your meals and company instead of moving quickly towards the next thing?

What if, just for today, you slowed it down to allow yourself more moments of peace in the in-between's— the little moments in between waking up and getting started with work. The small moments in between leaving and arriving.

What if, just for today, you allowed yourself just a few more slow moments to remember how precious this life really is. To remember that it all really, *really* is okay, even if it doesn't feel like it right now. What if you allowed yourself just a few moments to remember that in the big, *big* picture of this all, you are perfect. You are in perfect time and on the perfect path to where you are meant to go.

What if, just for today, you took it all just a little bit slower?

what if, just for today, you were entirely present?

What if, just for today, instead of thinking about tomorrow or the next day, you allowed yourself to deeply feel and experience everything that *this* day holds?

What if, just for today, instead of needing to know what will come next or what grand plan will follow this one, you allowed yourself to dive into the depths of *this* day?

What if, just for today, you allowed yourself the freedom of letting go of all of the questions you have about the future to just find love for the moment you are in?

What if, just for today, you worked on writing the story of today instead of worrying about the story of tomorrow?

What if, just for today, you allowed tomorrow to be tomorrow, and truly allowed today to be today?

The universe *already* has it all figured out for you. Things meant to be will come and things not meant to be will fall away. You are not supposed to know and understand every single thing that will happen or have all of your plans laid out. That is what makes life so wonderful and full of magic— that it isn't just about understanding or figuring it out. It is about *experiencing* it all deeply.

What if, just for today, you were entirely present?

Soul Waves

stillness and stars

Look up at the stars often.
Let them remind you what it means to be
powerful yet still.
Small yet significant.
Let them show you how they shine effortlessly
and remind you that you shine effortlessly, too—
just by being you.
Let them remind you
of your place in the world…
Let them remind you whenever you forget
that *you* belong here just as much as
every star belongs in the night sky.

for when there is too much going on at once

The moments when you have so many things going on at once are the moments that you need to pause and stop what you are doing the *most*. When you feel like you are juggling too many things in an impossible balancing act, *pause*.

When there are too many things going on at once, pausing might feel like the worst thing you could do because you do not have a moment to spare— but it is the *very thing* that will ground and center you again, allowing you to move ahead with a level head. Pausing during these moments will remind you that even when it feels like there isn't enough time, *there is*. It will remind you that yes, deadlines are important, but that it is also okay to take a moment to take a deep breath before you continue ahead... Pausing during these hectic moments or days or weeks will allow you to see all that you are doing in a different light. You might see that something does not actually need your attention right this moment. You might see that you could ask for help on something else. You might realize a solution in the stillness.

When there is too much going on all at once, *pause*. Give yourself a moment to clean your lens. A moment to welcome peace into your heart before you continue on.

Soul Waves

the way back to peace

You always have within you and with you
the way back towards peace:
your breath.

A reminder to return to this moment.
A gift of life. A gift from life.
A way to slow time.
A practice of feeling.
A practice of letting go.

It is with you, sweet soul.
It is within you.

Let your breath be the guide
for your days,
for your life.
It will always bring you home,
over and over and over.

on overthinking

Overthinking is exhausting—
Going in circles and circles,
Getting more overwhelmed with each one.

Stop. Pause. Breathe.

Let go and release—
Let go of all the things that you cannot control.
Release everything that was never yours to hold.

Pause and breathe—
Pause and realize that you don't need to know
everything. It is okay to be unsure and to not know.
Breathe deeply and welcome peace with each breath. All
is well.

Choose and act—
Choose *something* and know that making a decision is
better than delaying it. Do the best you can now and
know that it is enough.
Act and take a step forward bravely and confidently,
immediately.

slowing time

Slow time.
Be still.
Be here and now.
Be timeless.
Bring yourself back to *this* moment,
over and over and over again.

When the day is really busy.
When the day is really empty.
Bring yourself back to *this* moment,
over and over and over again.

When the day is really stressful.
When the day is overflowing with joy.
Bring yourself back to *this* moment,
over and over and over again.

When you are hurting, when your heart is heavy.
When you are in love, when your heart soars.
Bring yourself back to *this* moment,
over and over and over again.

Bring yourself back to this moment. As meditation. As
water for the soul. As healing. As medicine. As a practice
of presentness and peace. Bring yourself back to now. To
let go of tomorrow's stress. To release yesterday's pain.
To come back to the timeless, eternal moment of

now.

Because in the stillness of now,
you will find *all* that you are seeking.

VIII. Affirmations

affirmations introduction - the mind's garden

Reading, speaking, and declaring affirmations is, at its core, a practice of *tending to your thoughts*. If your inner world is a garden, speaking affirmations is a way of tending to the weeds, planting new seeds, and nurturing the existing blooms.

The weeds are negative, harmful, and often untrue thoughts— "I'll never be good enough," "I wish I was more like them," "My dreams are unrealistic. I can never make it," "It is too late to change."

One or two of these won't destroy a garden, but imagine the person who, every day, repeats these thoughts compared to the person whose garden is full of thoughts such as— "I am good enough, I deserve my place here," "There is no need to compare myself to anyone else. I have all of the gifts I need to live out my purpose." "What if I *could* do that hard thing?" You can imagine how different these two people's lives would be from the way they think about themselves and their world.

Over time, you begin to believe the things you repeatedly tell yourself— *regardless of how true they are*. This is why we must do the inner work of tending to our thoughts.

The following pages are words of kindness, truth, and love. Words that are medicine. Words that are healing. Words to help you through. Words to remind you of your power and your strength. Words to help you tend to your mind's garden.

May you read these affirmations slowly and feel them deeply. May these affirmations wash your soul clean and remind you of the truths that you have always known. May these words plant beautiful seeds in the garden of your mind.

affirmation for when your world is moving too fast

I am grounded in peace.

I breathe in a deep, full breath,
letting it fill every inch of my lungs.
I release it slowly.
All is calm, all is peace.
I am well. I am safe. I am at peace.

I am grounded in peace.

I am safe and secure in my being
and in my place in the world.
All of my needs are provided for.
I am exactly where I need to be
in this moment.
I am anchored and grounded in this
present moment where all is well
and all is moving in perfect time.
I give my all. I do not rush.
I am anchored and grounded in this
present moment where *I* am well.

I am grounded in peace.

affirmation for remembering your self worth

I am limitless. I am capable. I am strong.

I may have worries, but I am not my worries.
I may have troubles, but I am not my troubles.
I may have struggles, but I am not my struggles.

I am not my faults nor my past. I am not my pains nor my shortcomings.

I am so much more.

I am light. I am capable. I am complex and intricate. I am strong. I am beautiful. I am worthy.

I release my fear of not being good enough.
I release my uncertainties of the present and the future.
I release my doubts of what lies ahead.

I am limitless. I am capable. I am strong.

Soul Waves

affirmation for owning your worth

My worth comes from just one place: *within me*.
My worth does not come from my parents, my boss, my
coworkers, my friends, my teachers, nor my peers.

My worth comes from me.
I am as worthy as I let myself be.

My worth does not change depending on my success nor
my failures. It does not change depending on who sees it
in me. My worth is *inherent*.

I am *inherently* worthy of deep joy.
I am *inherently* worthy of boundless love.
I am *inherently* worthy of a peaceful heart.
I am *inherently* worthy of the good.

I am worthy of living out the life I dream of living.
I am worthy of my own love and kindness.
I am worthy of becoming all I dream of becoming.

affirmation for choosing thankfulness

Today, I'm choosing to be thankful for it all—
for the past, for everything that happens tomorrow, for
everything right in front of me today.

Today, I'm choosing to be thankful for the things I
wished happened differently. For the moments I wish I
acted differently. For the moments I succeeded. For the
moments I fell and lost my way. For the moments that I
felt on top of the whole world.

Today, I'm choosing to be thankful for *every* moment.
Today, I'm choosing to be thankful for every breath I
have taken and every breath I have yet to take.

Today, I'm choosing to be thankful for this beautiful life,
its messiness and magic and all.

affirmation for getting through this

I will rise. I will overcome.
I am getting through this.
I am overcoming this tough situation.

I know and trust that like the sun always rises again, I will rise again, too. These moments— whether hours, days, months, or years— are a part of my story, but they are *not* my entire story. There is so much more to me beyond this. I am getting through this. I am stronger than I know. I am learning how to overcome.

I release my hurts. I release my pain. I welcome peace and joy into my heart. I welcome healing into my soul. Even with all of this, there is peace in the world for me. There is love in the world for me. There is joy in the world for me.

I am okay, and sooner than I know, I will be *great* again, too. Sooner than I know, I will say:
I rose up. I overcame it all. I found my strength and I found my peace. I got through this. I am okay. I am blessed. I am joyful.

Nikki Banas

affirmation for remembering that it will be okay

On all days—
and especially on the days of doubts—
I remind myself that:
everything will be okay.

Not because it is easy to say
and not because I take the words lightly,
but because truly,
everything will be okay.

Every single storm comes to an end.
Every dark night eventually becomes day and
every long winter eventually becomes a warm,
beautiful summer.

I know that better moments are right around the corner.
I have made it through worse days and harder seasons. It
isn't always easy, but I always make it through, and I will
this time, too.

The way out is truly *through* so I breathe deeply and
remember that it will be okay. I will make it out stronger
and lighter. I release my fears and hold onto courage. I
do my best that I can today, no matter what that looks
like. *Everything will be okay.*

Soul Waves

affirmation for welcoming joy

I open my heart to the joy that is here for me right now.
I do not need to wait in order to be joyful,
tomorrow it will be too late to experience
all of the joys of today.

I embrace my current reality and
all the joys that it holds.
I work hard for where I dream of going,
but I do not stop myself from savoring all of the joy
along the way.

There are many gifts for me in this day and
it is up to me to let them touch my heart.
Whether it is the gift of the sunrise or someone to love,
a nurturing meal or a blooming rose,
a new show to watch or a good book to read,
time with a dear friend or cozy night inside,
I welcome the joys of this day into my heart
and let it fill me from the inside out.

affirmation for your energy and efforts

I am not blind to the flaws and faults of others,
the flaws and faults of myself,
nor my circumstances,
but I do not dwell in them.

I do not dwell on things that I cannot change.
I do not dwell on battles that are not mine to fight.
I do not dwell on things that do not deserve my energy.

My energy is limited and precious,
so I pour it into
the things I can change,
the ways I can grow,
those who I can help.

I pour it into
kindness, love, and grace.

affirmation for believing in the good

I believe in the good.
Good things are on their way.
I welcome good news,
good opportunities,
good blessings.

I open my heart to
receiving all of the good things that
are meant for me.
I am worthy. I am deserving.
I welcome the good in my life and
into the lives of others.

affirmation for experiencing this day deeply

This day is meant to be
deeply felt, loved, and experienced.

I welcome the joys of today into my heart and let them
ignite the fire within me. I celebrate this day as a piece of
the story of who I am.

I welcome love into my heart today— for myself, for the
ones around me, for the life that I am living.

I allow the stress of today to teach me greater patience
and strength. I do not let it consume me. Instead, I use it
to propel me forward.

Today may hold questions without answers, and it may
hold moments I do not understand. But I do not need to
have all of the answers to enjoy this day deeply. I trust
that answers to the questions I have will come in time. I
will live this day fully anyways.

This day is meant to be
deeply felt, loved, and experienced.
This day is a part of my story,
and I live it fully and entirely.

affirmation for welcoming a new month

I celebrate the month that just ended
with all love and gratitude.
Thank you for the blessings and the lessons.
The teachings and the joys.
The memories made and days spent well.
The days of rain and the days of shine.

Thank you for bringing me things that I didn't know I
needed and for new joys that I was not expecting.

I welcome the new month
with all love and gratitude.
I welcome the blessings and
open my heart to receive the joy and love that
this new month will bring.

I know that there will be
tough days and challenges,
growing pains, and plans that won't work out.
As I navigate through the month, I embrace the growth I
need to be able to overcome these tough moments.

I embrace the new month with an open heart and mind.
I am ready to continue my growth, live deeply, and
make brand new memories to cherish.

Nikki Banas

affirmation for accepting this moment

I am exactly where I need to be.

The universe has put me in *this* situation for a reason,
even if I do not understand the reason yet—
even if I never will understand the reason.

I am exactly where I need to be for
my growth, my happiness, my becoming,
and my journey.

It is up to me to embrace this moment for all that it is
instead of fighting its reality. There is something here for
me to learn. There is something here for me to embrace
with my heart. There is something here for me to find
peace in. There is so much for me here. I allow new
perspectives through the words, thoughts, and energies
around me to open my eyes and heart to this moment
and this place that I am in.

I am grounded, secure, and strong, here and now. There
are blessings around me and I open my eyes and my
heart to receiving them.

I am exactly where I need to be.

affirmation for welcoming love

Today, I am letting go of all of the 'should have beens'
and am embracing everything that is.

Today, I am letting go of how I thought it would be and
embracing how it is.

Today, I am grateful for how it all is.
Even if I wished it would be different.
Even if I never thought I would be here.
I am grateful for how it is and where I am.

Today, I am embracing all that is right in front of me
with love, gratitude, acceptance, and joy.
Because, there really is *so much* good
right in front of me—
there is so much to love right here,
in this moment.

And today, *I am choosing to love it all.*

affirmation for giving love

I spread love everywhere I go.
I am a light to others.
The impact of my love goes further
than I will ever know.

I am kind.
I am compassionate.
I care about others and their well being.

I do not hold back my love.
Giving love tomorrow is too late.
I   love   today.
I am kind today.
I am compassionate today.
I am understanding today.
I give grace today.
I give love today.

affirmation for believing in yourself

I wholeheartedly believe in
myself, my capabilities, and my growth.
I believe in my strength and my ability to learn.
I believe in my dreams.
I believe in my goals and the plans that I make.
I know that I will overcome every obstacle and that I will
become stronger every time that I do.
I give it my all every day,
and know that in time,
I will get to where I dream of going.

affirmation on moving in perfect time

There is no rush.
There is no race.
There is no need to worry or to
compare where I am to where anyone else is.

I am right on time.
I am moving at the right pace for
my unique journey through life.

I release my anxiety to the skies and
allow trust and faith to fill my heart that
I am in perfect time.

I surrender to the unknowing of all that is ahead of me,
and know that the unfolding of life is what makes its
journey so beautiful to live out.

I release my timelines and my urgency of the future to
welcome peace into this moment.

I release the need of knowing what is to come to focus on
experiencing all that this moment holds just for me.

Soul Waves

affirmation for never giving up on yourself

I never give up on myself.
I believe in myself and my ability to stand up,
again and again and again and again.

I never give up on myself.
I fight for who I am and all that I believe in.
I am focused on my purpose because
I am here to live out my purpose.

I never give up on myself.
Even if someone else gives up on me,
I never give up on myself.

I never give up on myself.
I always try.
I always brush myself off and stand back up when I fall.
Every single time.

I know there will be
setbacks and heartaches and hurts along the way,
but I never let anyone or anything out there keep me
from believing in and standing up for
myself, my power, and my purpose.

affirmation for planting the seeds of your future

I hold the seeds of my future so
I plant the seeds that I want to see grow.

I plant seeds of joy, seeds of purpose, seeds of love.
I plant the seeds of my dreams.

I have full trust and faith in the seeds that I sow, and
know that in perfect time, they will bloom.

My thoughts, my words, and my actions are all in
alignment with my growth and becoming.

Soul Waves

affirmation for aligning with your true path

I am in alignment with my true self and my true path.
I am moving at the perfect pace.
I am patient in knowing that my hard work is paying off,
I am determined to continue taking steps that will propel
me forward.

I trust that I am on the path that will lead me towards
where I am meant to go in perfect time— even, and
especially, when I cannot fully understand the place that
I am in.

I trust and honor my journey.
I trust my intuition and allow it to guide me forward.
I know that every twist and turn is a part of my path.
I am full of peace in knowing that no day is ever wasted
in my journey. Every twist and turn is helping me grow.

I honor my journey by
giving my best that I can every day.
My journey honors me by
taking me everywhere that I am destined to go.

affirmation for being the author of your own life

I am the author of my life and the creator of my future.
I hold the pen to the story of my life.

I write the story that I want to read.
I write the story of the life that I have always dreamed of.

I write of overcoming my obstacles.
I write of bringing my dreams to life.

I write what I want to see happen in my life. I work on my dreams and I believe in my ability to bring my dreams into fruition.

affirmation for living your purpose

I have a purpose.
I have all that I need to live and fulfill my purpose.
The tools, the skills, the character.
I am worthy of living my purpose and
I am worthy of following my calling.
When I feel a dream stirring within me,
I honor it.
I trust that my intuition is leading me towards
my greatest gifts.
My purpose is a gift from the universe,
and my gift to the universe is following my purpose.

Nikki Banas

affirmation for expansion

The life around me is full of so many wonders.
People, music, literature, art, animals,
plants, ideas, dreams, places.
I give myself time to follow my curiosities
everywhere they take me.
Whether to a new city or
within the pages of a new book,
I go wherever I feel a pull.

My life is constantly
growing and expanding
with new possibilities
and new growth.
The universe is ever expanding, and *so I am.*

affirmation for embracing your authentic self

I shine so bright, just as I am.
I allow my guard to come down.
I express my feelings, my thoughts, and my love freely.
I do not need to hide who I am or
try to be like anyone else.
I allow the unfiltered me to shine bright.
I am at my best when I am entirely *myself.*

I shine so bright, just as I am.
I allow myself to grow, change, and bloom—
over and over again into new versions of myself.
I release old versions of me who I no longer am.
I celebrate all versions of myself because they are all a
part of my beautiful evolution.

I shine so bright, just as I am.
I am confident in who I am.
I believe in who I am.
I celebrate myself and all that I am.
I release any other's opinions to the skies—
their opinions were never mine to hold anyway.

I embrace all that I have been,
all that I am,
and all that I am becoming.

affirmation for owning your space

I deserve to be here.
I do not need to be flawless or
perfect to have a place here.
I do not need to know everything or
have it all figured out already.

I deserve to be here.
I am confident in my abilities.
I trust in my ability to learn.
I trust in my ability to grow and adapt.
I am proud of who I am.
I celebrate all of the work I have put in to get here.

I deserve to be here.
I own my space.
I do not need to shallow myself or
make myself smaller to fit in.
I am proud of who I am.
I am authentically *me.*

affirmation for loving your authentic self

I accept myself fully and love myself entirely for who I am. Confidence radiates from my heart and I allow myself to feel worthy and loved exactly as I am.

I am not blind to my flaws, but I know that my worth is not tied to my flaws nor mistakes. I am worthy just as I am.

I am confident. I am beautiful. I am divine.
I am proud of who I am.

I trust myself as the oceans trust the moon.
I allow myself to shine bright like
the night sky does the stars.
I have faith in myself and my dreams like
the flowers hold faith in the sun.

I accept myself, my strengths, my flaws,
my past, my triumphs, my talents.
I accept and cherish myself—
entirely.

affirmation for moving through change with grace

I allow myself to shift with the seasons.
I allow myself to ebb and flow through
different times of my life.
I allow myself to go through
cycles and phases like the sun and moon.

I move with grace through
my own seasons of life—
Seasons of rest.
Seasons of planting.
Seasons of growing.
Seasons of blooming.
Seasons of harvest.

I do not force growth in times when my soul yearns for
rest. I do not force myself to bloom when my roots need
nourishment.

I embrace *this* season, in all that it holds for me. Whether
rest or harvest, I embrace this season for all that it is.

Soul Waves

affirmation for closed doors

It is okay if a door closes for me.
It is okay if I am facing an ending
that I did not expect to face.
It is okay if I feel like I am starting all over.

Every door I walk through will not be for me and that is
okay, because the ones that close are guiding me towards
the ones that *are* meant for me and my journey.

Sometimes it takes time to see a new door opening.
Sometimes it takes time to understand
why a door had to close.
I am patient. I am grateful while I wait.
I keep my eyes and heart open to
new opportunities in unexpected places.
I stay in joy, knowing that no door ever closes
without a new one opening.

Even if I cannot see the way right now,
I know that I am on my way towards
all that is meant for me.

affirmation for feeling anxious

I am not my thoughts.
I am not my fears.
I am not my worries.
I am not my troubles.
I am not the pressure I feel.

I slow down.
I breathe deeply and
s l o w l y.

I welcome peace.
I welcome stillness.
I welcome calmness.

I am more than my thoughts.
I am more than my fears.
I am more than my worries.
I am more than my troubles.
I am more than my anxiety.
I am so much more.

I am peaceful.
I am still.
I am calm.
I am well.

Soul Waves

affirmation for peace in the waves of your soul

Before all else, I fill my heart with peace.
Before I need to make a big decision.
Before I have an important conversation.
Before I make a big choice.
Before I jump in to my work.
Before I help those around me.
Before I begin a new day.
Before I shut my eyes at the end of the day.

I honor myself first with a moment of peace.
I soften my shoulders.
I release the tension I have been holding onto.
The tension in my forehead, my shoulders, my neck,
my hands, my stomach.
I fill every corner of my lungs with a fresh breath.
I breathe in peace.

I forgive those who I need to forgive.
I breathe in peace. I breathe out all of my hurts.
I release all that is not mine to hold.

Before all else, I allow peace to wash over me and calm the
waters within me.

In all that I do, I do it with a heart full of peace.

may you always find peace
within the waves of your soul.

Index by Piece Title

Meet the Author

Author and creator, Nikki Banas found her love for writing at a young age. After receiving a journal as a gift as a young girl, she discovered so much joy and freedom within its blank pages. Many years later, Nikki began sharing her letters of encouragement under the name *Walk the Earth* on Instagram and Pinterest, touching the hearts of many with her raw, honest, and encouraging words.

Nikki resides outside of Chicago and spends her time writing, exploring nature, and being with her family.

You can purchase her books on Amazon, as well as other treasures with her writing at: NikkiBanas.com. You can connect with her on Instagram and Pinterest @WalkTheEarthWriter.

Other Books by Nikki Banas

Printed in Great Britain
by Amazon

66530705R00106